Love

&

Hate

for Allaah's Sake

by
Shaykh Saleem al-Hilaalee

Translated by
Aboo Talhah Daawood ibn Ronald Burbank

ISBN 1 898649 09 X

British Library Cataloguing in Publication Data.

A catalogue record for this book is available from the British Library.

First Edition, 1416 AH/1995 CE

Cover design: Abu Yahya

Typeset by: Al-Hidaayah Publishing and Distribution

Published by: Al-Hidaayah Publishing and Distribution
                     P.O. Box 3332
                     Birmingham
                     United Kingdom
                     B10 0UH

                     Tel: 0121 753 1889
                     Fax: 0121 753 2422

Email: mail@al-hidaayah.co.uk

Publisher's Note

All praise is for Allaah, Lord of the worlds. Peace and prayers be upon Muhammad, his family, his Companions and all those who follow in their footsteps until the Last Day.

It gives us great pleasure in presenting the first English translation of *Al-Hubbu wal-Bughdu Fillaah* by Shaykh Saleem al-Hilaalee, the notable student of Shaykh Naasiruddeen al-Albaanee.

We pray that through this book Allaah guides our hearts to loving and hating for His sake alone, so that we may taste the sweetness of *eemaan*, and experience the delight of true brotherhood. We ask that He makes us from amongst those who will be under His shade on the Day when there will be no shade except His - *aameen.*

Al-Hidaayah Publishing and Distribution

Please note that all the references that have been quoted refer to the Arabic books unless otherwise stated.

Contents

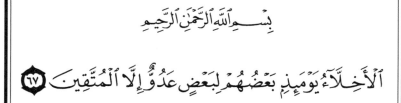

بِسْمِ اللَّهِ الرَّحْمَنِ الرَّحِيمِ

ٱلْأَخِلَّآءُ يَوْمَئِذٍ بَعْضُهُمْ لِبَعْضٍ عَدُوٌّ إِلَّا ٱلْمُتَّقِينَ ﴿٦٧﴾

"Friends that Day will be foes one to another except the
pious who fear Allaah (*al-Muttaqoon*)."

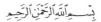

Introduction

All praise is for Allaah, we praise Him, we seek His aid and we ask for His forgiveness. We seek Allaah's refuge from the evil within ourselves and from our evil actions. Whomsoever Allaah guides then none can misguide him, and whomsoever Allaah misguides then none can guide him. I testify that none has the right to be worshipped except Allaah, and I testify that Muhammad is His Slave and Messenger.

Loving and hating for Allaah is one of the great doors leading to the good of the Hereafter and a cause of tasting the sweetness of *eemaan* in this world. There are some people who think that loving and hating is an affair of the heart only and that a person is unable to have any control over it, so how is he able to cause himself to love one and to hate another?!

From that which is known necessarily in Islaam is that the heart is to follow *'aqeedah* and *eemaan*, so whoever has *eemaan* in Allaah as his Lord, Islaam as his religion and way of life (*Deen*) and in Muhammad (ﷺ) as the Messenger, then he must necessarily love whoever loves Allaah, therefore loving and hating for Allaah is an obligation upon the Muslim.

Furthermore, Allaah, the Most High, has warned us against going beyond bounds in these two matters so that we do not cause dissension and widespread corruption in the land, as occurs at the end of *Sooratul-Anfaal:*

وَٱلَّذِينَ كَفَرُوا بَعْضُهُمْ أَوْلِيَآءُ بَعْضٍ إِلَّا تَفْعَلُوهُ تَكُن فِتْنَةٌ فِى ٱلْأَرْضِ وَفَسَادٌ كَبِيرٌ ۝

"And those who disbelieve are allies to one another, and if you (the Muslims) do not do so, there will be *fitnah* (wars, battles, polytheism etc.) and oppression on the earth, and a great mischief and corruption (appearance of polytheism)."

al-Anfaal (8):73

7

Allaah, the Magnificent, has guided us and likewise His Messenger (ﷺ), to the correct way of loving and hating for Allaah, which if followed will lead us to the shaded oasis of *eemaan* and security.

Here for you, O brother, is an explanation of its signposts in the light of the Noble Qur'aan and the authentic *Sunnah* that it may become as clear as dawn for those who love one another for Allaah's sake and those who form ties and strive and sacrifice in that for Him, so that their bonds of mutual love are strong and the ties between them in their *da'wah* remain firm, so that they are brothers for Allaah's sake and they unite and help one another upon the way prescribed by Allaah, clinging to it with their molars - to both the *Sunnah* and the Qur'aan.

I ask Allaah through my love for Him and for His Messenger (ﷺ) and for those who love them that He harmonises the hearts of the Muslims upon the true *Deen* and that He accepts this with a favourable acceptance so that it may be a guide for those who love each other for Allaah's Majesty, guiding to that which is correct in the manner that is best.

Further, I hope that my earnest and sincere brother who finds good in it will praise Allaah and not forget us when making righteous supplication, and if he finds other than that, then let him not hesitate to advise since I am attentive and ready to listen. It is Allaah who guides to the right way.

Written by:

Aboo Usaamah Saleem ibn 'Eed al-Hilaalee
2nd. Ramadaan al-Mubaarak 1408 from the *Hijrah* of Allaah's Messenger Muhammad (ﷺ).
Amaan, the capital of Jordan.

What is Loving and Hating for the Sake of Allaah?

Love is having affection and hating is its opposite. A person may love another for their wealth, or beauty, or honour or lineage, or for personal gain, or for a worldly desire or fleeting aim. All of these reasons are detestable in Islaam which has laid down the reasons for loving and hating - and it is the *Deen*.

Therefore the Muslim does not love a person except for the correctness of his *Deen*, and does not hate a person except for the corruption of his *Deen*. He (ﷺ) said: *"There are three characteristics whoever has them will find the sweetness of eemaan: That Allaah and His Messenger are more beloved to him than all else; that he loves a person and does not love him except for Allaah; and that he would hate to revert to unbelief just as he would hate to be thrown into the fire."*[1]

Therefore the Muslim loves the prophets, the righteous ones loved by Allaah, the sincere followers of the prophets, the martyrs and the pious - since they carry out that which Allaah loves, so he loves them for Allaah and this is from the completion of his love for Allaah since loving the beloved of the one that you love is from the completion of love for the one that you love. Further, he hates the unbelievers, the hypocrites and the people of innovation and sin, since they do that which Allaah hates so he hates them for Allaah.

---

[1] Reported by al-Bukhaaree (1/60 of *al-Fath*) and Muslim (2/13-14 of an-Nawawee) from the *hadeeth* of Anas ibn Maalik, *radiyallaahu 'anhu*.

So whoever does this has loved for Allaah and hated for Allaah and Allaah is sufficient for him and is the most excellent Protector.

Know that loving for Allaah and hating for Allaah is not the same as alliance (*walaa'*) with the Believers and separating oneself (*baraa'*) from the polytheists (*mushriks*), but rather it differs in that:

(a) Alliance and separation (*al-walaa' wal baraa'*) is the foundation, and loving and hating is a matter from its completion.
(b) Loving and hating necessarily follows on from alliance and separation - and not the opposite.

Why Should Loving and Hating be for Allaah's Sake Alone?

(1) FROM THE COMPLETION OF A PERSON'S LOVE FOR HIS LORD AND FOR THE MESSENGER OF ALLAAH (ﷺ) IS THAT HE LOVES THAT WHICH ALLAAH LOVES.

He loves a person for Allaah's sake and not for any other reason so one who loves the prophets and the righteous because of their carrying out those things loved by Allaah, not for anything else, then he has indeed loved for Allaah alone and not for sake of other than Him. However many people are not pleased with Allaah alone as their Guardian and Helper, rather they take for themselves protectors and helpers other than Him, loving them just as they love Allaah, thinking that they will bring them closer to Allaah. Their taking them as protectors and patrons is the same as taking the protection and patronage of those close to an (earthly) king and this is nothing but *shirk*. Whereas *tawheed* is that you do not take any protectors and patrons besides Allaah, and the Qur'aan and the *Sunnah* are replete with descriptions of the *mushriks* as being people who take protectors and patrons besides Him. Furthermore, this is a different matter to having love for and allying oneself with His prophets, messengers and believing servants for His sake since this is from the completion of *eemaan* and a completion of taking Him as ones Patron and Protector. This is because having love for and allying oneself with those whom He loves is one thing, whereas taking one whom He loves to be a patron and a protector besides Him is something quite different. Indeed one who does not understand the clear difference between the two should seek to discover *tawheed* afresh since this affair is the very root of *tawheed* and the central pivot of Islaam.

(2) ALLAAH, THE ONE FREE OF ALL DEFECTS AND THE MOST HIGH, THROUGH HIS MERCY, GATHERED THE HEARTS OF THE BELIEVERS UPON OBEDIENCE TO HIM, AND UNITED THEM UPON THE WAY (*MANHAJ*) WHICH HE PRESCRIBED, THEREFORE HE, THE ONE FREE FROM ALL IMPERFECTIONS, DESERVES TO BE THANKED FOR THIS GREAT FAVOUR, SO THAT ONE LOVES FOR HIS SAKE ALONE AND CLINGS ONTO HIS FIRM ROPE.

Allaah, the Most High, says:

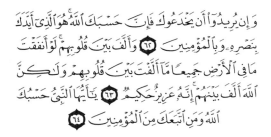

"And if they intend to deceive you, then verily, Allaah is All-Sufficient for you. He it is who has supported you with His Help and with the believers. And he has united their (the believer's) hearts. If you had spent all that is in the earth, you could not have united their hearts, but Allaah has united them. Certainly He is All-Mighty, All-Wise. O Prophet (Muhammad (ﷺ)) Allaah is sufficient for you and for the believers who follow you."

al-Anfaal (8):62-64

This miracle, possible only for Allaah, occurred, and it could occur only with this *'aqeedah*. These hearts which were averse and these headstrong dispositions changed and they became a closely united group of amenable brothers, loving one another and united in a companionship of a level unknown in history, the like of which has not been known upon the earth.

Indeed this *'aqeedah* is truly a source of amazement. When it enters the hearts it produces a mixture of love, companionship and affection between hearts which it causes to become tender and sensitive, it ties them with a bond that is strong, pro-

12

found and gentle. So that the glance of an eye, the touch of the hand, and the beat of the heart contain realities of mutual compassion and mutual acquaintance, mutual friendship and alliance, mutual aid, liberality and forbearance whose secret is not known except by the One who through His Mercy united these hearts, and these things are not experienced except by these hearts.

This 'aqeedah never ceases to call the people with the call of love for Allaah's sake, so that when they respond to that which gives them life - that miracle, whose secret is known to Allaah alone and over which none but Allaah has any power, is brought about. Allaah, the Magnificent, says:

$$\text{وَٱعْتَصِمُوا بِحَبْلِ ٱللَّهِ جَمِيعًا وَلَا تَفَرَّقُوا}$$
$$\text{وَٱذْكُرُوا نِعْمَتَ ٱللَّهِ عَلَيْكُمْ إِذْ كُنتُمْ أَعْدَآءً فَأَلَّفَ بَيْنَ قُلُوبِكُمْ}$$
$$\text{فَأَصْبَحْتُم بِنِعْمَتِهِ إِخْوَانًا وَكُنتُمْ عَلَىٰ شَفَا حُفْرَةٍ مِّنَ ٱلنَّارِ}$$
$$\text{فَأَنقَذَكُم مِّنْهَا كَذَٰلِكَ يُبَيِّنُ ٱللَّهُ لَكُمْ ءَايَٰتِهِ لَعَلَّكُمْ تَهْتَدُونَ}$$

"And hold fast, all of you together, to the Rope of Allaah, and be not divided among yourselves, and remember Allaah's favour upon you, for you were enemies one to another, but He joined your hearts together, so that, by His Grace, you became brothers, and you were on the brink of a pit of Fire, and He saved you from it. Thus Allaah makes His Signs clear to you, that you may be guided."

Aal-'Imraan (3):103

So Allaah, the One free of all imperfections, mentions two supporting pillars: the first being Islaam, and the second being brotherhood for Allaah's sake, upon the way and methodology prescribed by Allaah in order for the methodology prescribed by Allaah to be fulfilled. So it is a brotherhood proceeding from the first supporting pillar of *taqwaa* and Islaam; its foundation is clinging to the Rope of Allaah, and it is not merely a gathering together on any other shape, form or conception, nor for any other goal, nor by means of any other rope - from the many different ropes which will only cause separation. It can be nothing but Islaam which will join these hearts that are averse to one another, and it will only be the Rope of Allaah which all will cling onto together, thus becoming brothers by Allaah's favour, and nothing but love for Allaah's sake will gather the hearts - since all historical grudges, all tribal feuds, personal greed, and ignorant nationalistic banners will come to nothing, but the row will be well ordered beneath the banner of Allaah, the True, the Most Great and the Most High. You will see those who had love for one another due to the light and guidance which Allaah gave them, not due to any kinds of kinship, nor due to wealth or trade.

This is witnessed to by the fact that the divinely guided *ummah* (nation) which Allaah's Messenger (ﷺ) built upon loving and hating for Allaah's sake was not merely sweet words or idealistic actions for individuals, but rather it was a lofty and practical reality built upon this firm foundation, none having the ability to unite the hearts like this but Him.

(3) THE *DEEN* PRESCRIBED BY ALLAAH, THE ONE FREE FROM ALL IMPERFECTIONS, ALONE IS THAT WHICH WILL SET THE FEET FIRMLY, BIND THE HEARTS AND BRING TOGETHER UPON THE WORD OF *TAWHEED*, SINCE IT IS THE WAY TO UNITY. WHEREAS THE SHORT-LIVED WORLDLY AFFAIRS , PERSONAL AMBITIONS, WORLDLY INTERESTS AND MATTERS RELATING TO OWNERSHIP OF LAND WILL ONLY IMPEDE AND NOT CAUSE UNION, CAUSE CONFLICT AND NOT HARMONY, AND WILL CAUSE DISUNITY AND NOT RECONCILIATION.

Allaah, the Most High, says:

$$وَأَنَّ هَٰذَا صِرَٰطِى مُسْتَقِيمًا فَٱتَّبِعُوهُ وَلَا تَتَّبِعُوا۟ ٱلسُّبُلَ فَتَفَرَّقَ بِكُمْ عَن سَبِيلِهِۦ ۚ ذَٰلِكُمْ وَصَّىٰكُم بِهِۦ لَعَلَّكُمْ تَتَّقُونَ ﴿١٥٣﴾$$

"And verily, this is My Straight Path, so follow it, and follow not (other) paths, for they will separate you from His Path. This He has ordained for you that you may attain piety."

al-An'aam (6):153

So this is Allaah's Path, and the way which He prescribed and there is besides it nothing except the other divergent paths which cause separation between those who follow them and deviate from the plain and clear guidance. This is the Divine Guidance given to mankind that they may become people of *taqwaa*. So it is *taqwaa* which will lead the hearts to the Clear Way and bind them with the bond of love, harmony and affection, otherwise affection will become enmity, and love will become hatred.

14

Allaah, the Most High, says:

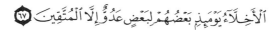

"Friends that Day will be foes one to another except the pious who fear Allaah (al-Muttaqoon)."

az-Zukhruf (43):67

Indeed the enmity between these friends springs from the source of their worldly love of one another since they united upon evil, and were indulgent with regard to one another's misguidance. So on that Day they will blame one another for the consequences of their misguidance and the result of their evil. On that Day they will become adversaries heaping abuse on one another when once they had been friends who exchanged secrets. On that Day the oppressor who loved unjustifiably will bite his hand in regret, remorse and distress - and regret will be of no benefit then.

"And (remember) the Day when the wrongdoer will bite at his hands, he will say: 'Oh! Would that I had taken a path with the Messenger (Muhammad (ﷺ)). Ah! Woe to me! Would that I had never taken so-and-so as a friend! He indeed led me astray from the Reminder (the Qur'aan) after it had come to me. And Satan is ever a deserter to man in the hour of need.'"

al-Furqaan (25): 27-29

All his friends round about will be silent as he raises his grieving voice in mournful tones, but no one will respond to him, he has lost every loved one and close friend, so he begins to bite his hands in regret, remorse and sorrow... and biting on one hand will not suffice him, rather he bites one and then the other or both together due to his severe anguish.

Whilst the former friends are lost in their recriminations and their regrets, those who loved one another for Allaah's sake and formed ties for Him and were sincere towards each other will be surrounded with security, calm and tranquillity.

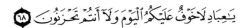

"My worshippers! No fear shall be on you this Day nor shall you grieve."

az-Zukhruf (43):68

'O Allaah, gather our hearts upon your prescribed way, and make us from those who love You, and from those who love those who love You, since we know that a person will be raised up along with those he loves.'

From Anas ibn Maalik who said that a man said to the Prophet (ﷺ), *"When will the Hour be, O Messenger of Allaah?" He replied, "What have you prepared for it?" He said: "I have not prepared for it a great deal of prayer, fasting or charity, but I love Allaah and His Messenger." He (ﷺ) said, "You will be with those whom you love."*[2]

---

[2] Reported by al-Bukhaaree [Eng. trans. 8/123-124/no.192] Muslim [Eng.trans. 4/1386/no. 6378] and others, and there are similar narrations from 'Abdullaah ibn Mas'ood, Aboo Moosa al-Ash'aree and Safwaan ibn 'Assaal, *radiyallaahu 'anhum.*

$$\text{أَمْ حَسِبْتُمْ أَن تُتْرَكُوا۟ وَلَمَّا يَعْلَمِ ٱللَّهُ ٱلَّذِينَ جَهَدُوا۟}$$
$$\text{مِنكُمْ وَلَمْ يَتَّخِذُوا۟ مِن دُونِ ٱللَّهِ وَلَا رَسُولِهِۦ وَلَا ٱلْمُؤْمِنِينَ}$$
$$\text{وَلِيجَةً ۚ وَٱللَّهُ خَبِيرٌۢ بِمَا تَعْمَلُونَ ﴿١٦﴾}$$

"Do you think that you shall be left alone while He has not yet tested those among you who have striven hard and fought and have not taken *waleejah* (helpers, advisors and consultants from the disbelievers, pagans etc. giving openly to them their secrets) besides Allaah and His Messenger, and the Believers. Allaah is Well-Acquainted with what you do."

at-Tawbah (9):16

He (ﷺ) said: *"There are seven whom Allaah will shade in His shade[3] on the Day when there is no shade except His shade: The just ruler; a youth who grew up upon the worship of His Lord; a man whose heart is attached to the mosques;* **two men who love each other only for Allaah's sake - meeting and parting for that***; a man whom a woman of noble birth and beauty calls to commit fornication but he (refuses) and says: "I fear Allaah"; a man who gives charity secretly so that his left hand does not know what his right hand gives; and a man who remembers Allaah in private and his eyes flood with tears."[4]*

What is adhered to, always, is the correct methodology of Islaam... that which Allaah prescribed and which was shown to us in practical and exemplary form by the life of Allaah's Messenger (ﷺ), that is the criterion, and adherence is not to lineage, or individuals, or groups, or parties, or *madhhabs*, or sects, or governments, or nations. Indeed the shortcomings and weaknesses that have penetrated Islamic life are due to obstinacy and deviation from this criterion, or attempts to snatch this away from the hand of the Muslim worshipper... and instead of it infallibility is falsely attributed to persons given the status of holiness, who are raised above any criticism or error, and laughable excuses are invented to cover and explain their prac-

---

[3] i.e. the shade of His Throne (*'Arsh*) as shown in a version of a *hadeeth*, see *Fathul-Baaree* (2/144).

[4] Reported by al-Bukhaaree [Eng. trans. 1/356/no.629] and the wording is his, and Muslim [Eng. trans. 2/493/no.2248] from the *hadeeth* of Aboo Hurairah, *radiyallaahu 'anhu*.

tices and their errors which totally conflict with what Allaah loves and is pleased with, and have no connection at all with the correct methodology of Islaam. This is where failure and downfall begins - when the true Islamic goals and values are used to serve ones own ends.

All praise is for Allaah who gave one the wisdom to say:
"Indeed I will make it common to all,
         which is something the party makes forbidden:
How wretched, the afflictions of our *ummah*,
         That Islaam is made to serve an organisation."

This is when judgments begin to be passed according to who is the person in question, and means of bypassing the truth are extended to the point that whole works are written about them.

It is not fitting for the servant who loves Allaah, and loves and hates for Allaah's sake, and gives for Allaah, and withholds for Allaah, and forms ties for Allaah, and breaks ties for Allaah to think that calling to and clinging to the correct Islamic methodology with regard to alliance, loving and hating, and to avoid clinging to individuals, symbols and signs, will mean a return to disunity and mean that our efforts have been wasted.

Indeed this principle which binds the connection between the Muslims is not something about which we have a choice, rather it is something essential for the correction of the direction of Muslim society and for the ending of the man-made feudalism afflicting the life of the Muslims, so that what is adhered to is the Islaam which the Lord of the Worlds is pleased with as our *Deen*, as explained fully by Allaah's Messenger (ﷺ).

(2) Spreading the greeting of *Salaam*.

Know, O servant of Allaah, that greeting with *salaam* removes any feeling of alienation or fear and hearts therefore come together for Allaah's sake, he (ﷺ) said:
*"You will not enter Paradise until you believe (have eemaan), and you will not
believe (have eemaan) until you love one another. Shall I not guide you to something which if you carry out you will love one another. Spread as-Salaam amongst
yourselves."*[8]

(3) Giving Gifts.

He (ﷺ) said: *"Give gifts and you will love one another."*[9]

(4) Visiting.

Know, O brother, that visiting someone too frequently will cause him to tire of it,
the more frequently that one visits then the more tired of it he will become. Likewise visiting but seldomly will be insufficient and will lead to hardening of the hearts.
Therefore visit your brother now and again. He (ﷺ) said: *"Visit now and again -
your love will increase."*[10]

All praise is due to Allaah who gave one the wisdom to say:
"Visit now and again for it,
     If it is done too frequently will lead to abandonment:
For I have seen the people always weary of the rain
     Yet seeking it with raised hands when it is withheld."

---

[8] Reported be Muslim [Eng. trans. 1/37/no.96] and others from the *hadeeth* of Aboo Hurairah,
radiyallaahu 'anhu.

[9] Reported by al-Bukhaaree in *al-Adaabul-Mufrad* (no.594), ad-Doolaabee in *al-Kunaa* (1/150) and (2/
7), al-Baihaqee (6/169) and others. Its *isnaad* is *hasan*.

[10] *Saheeh*; reported by al-Bazzaar and others: *Saheehul-Jaami'*.

Likewise, one of them said:
"Limit the visits to your friend -
       You will be like a garment newly worn,
And the most tiresome thing for a person -
       Is that he always finds you with him."

(5) MODERATION IN LOVE AND HATRED.

He (ﷺ) said: *"Love the one whom you love in moderation perhaps one day he will be one whom you hate, and hate the one whom you hate in moderation perhaps one day he will be one whom you love."*[11]

So we find that taking the middle course involves all aspects of Islaam even with regards to feelings, emotions and affections. Therefore 'Umar ibn al-Khattaab said: "O Aslam do not love beyond due bounds, nor hate maliciously." He asked, "How is that?" He replied, "When you love then do not be like a child besotted with something, and if you hate then do not hate to the extent that you wish your companion to perish and be destroyed."[12]

Hudbah ibn Khashram said:
"And when you hate then hate moderately -
       For you do not know when you will have to return,
And be a source of good and pardon ill-treatment -
       For you will see and hear whatever you have done,
And when you love then love moderately
       For you do not know when you will be snatched away."

---

[11] *Saheeh*, see *Saheehul-Jaami'* (no.176). Reported by at-Tirmidhee and others. Also see *Ghaayatul-Maraam* (no.472).

[12] Reported by al-Bukhaaree in *al-Adaabul-Mufrad* (no.1322), 'Abdur-Razzaaq in *al-Musannaf* (no.30269) and al-Baghawee in *Sharhus-Sunnaah* (13/65). Its *isnaad* is *saheeh*.

(2) THOSE WHO HAVE MUTUAL LOVE FOR ALLAAH'S SAKE WILL BE UNDER THE SHADE OF THE THRONE OF THE MOST MERCIFUL (AR-RAHMAAN) ON THE DAY WHEN THERE WILL BE NO SHADE EXCEPT HIS SHADE.

He (ﷺ) said: *"Allaah will say on the Day of Resurrection: Where are those who had mutual love for my Glory's sake. Today I will shade them in my shade on the Day when there is no shade except My shade..."*[16]

(3) THOSE WHO HAVE MUTUAL LOVE FOR ALLAAH'S SAKE WILL BE UPON PILLARS OF LIGHT ON THE DAY OF RESURRECTION.

He (ﷺ) says in what he reports from his Lord: *"Allaah, the Mighty and Magnificent, says: Those who have mutual love for the sake of my Glory will have pillars of light and will be envied by the prophets and martyrs."*[17]

(4) THOSE WHO HAVE MUTUAL LOVE FOR ALLAAH'S SAKE WILL HAVE NO FEAR, NOR WILL THEY GRIEVE.

He (ﷺ) said: *"Indeed from the servants of Allaah there are some who are not prophets, yet they will be envied by the prophets and martyrs."* It was said, *"Who are they, that we may love them?"* He (ﷺ) said, *"They are people who have mutual love through light from Allaah, not due to kinship or ancestry, their faces will be enlightened, upon pillars of light, they will not fear when the people fear, nor grieve when the people grieve."* Then he (ﷺ) recited:

$$ أَلَا إِنَّ أَوْلِيَاءَ اللَّهِ لَا خَوْفٌ عَلَيْهِمْ وَلَا هُمْ يَحْزَنُونَ $$

"No doubt! Verily, on the friends (*awliyaa'*) of Allaah there is no fear, nor shall they grieve." [Soorah Yoonus (10):62] [18]

---

[16] Reported by Muslim [Eng. trans 4/1362/no.6225] from the *badeeth* of Aboo Hurairah, *radiyallaahu 'anhu.*

[17] Reported by at-Tirmidhee [no.2390] and Ahmad [5/236-237]. Its *isnaad* is *saheeh*.

[18] Reported by Ibn Hibbaan (*al-Mawaarid* no.2508) from the *badeeth* of Aboo Hurairah with *hasan isnaad.*

(5) LOVING FOR ALLAAH'S SAKE LEADS TO TASTING THE SWEETNESS OF *EEMAAN*.

He (ﷺ) said: *"Whoever would like to taste the sweetness of eemaan then let him love a person, not loving him except for Allaah's sake."*[19]

(6) LOVING AND HATING FOR ALLAAH'S SAKE IS FROM THE COMPLETION OF *EEMAAN*.

He (ﷺ) said: *"He who loves for Allaah and hates for Allaah; and gives for Allaah and withholds for Allaah - has perfected eemaan."*[20]

(7) LOVING FOR ALLAAH'S SAKE LEADS TO PARADISE.

He (ﷺ) said: *"You will not enter Paradise until you believe (have eemaan) and you will not believe until you have mutual love. Shall I not guide you to something which if you carry out you will have love for one another. Spread (the greeting of) 'as-Salaam' amongst yourselves."*[21]

---

[19] Reported by Ahmad [2/298], al-Haakim [1/3 and 4/168] and others. From Aboo Hurirah, *radiyallaahu 'anhu*, and its *isnaad* is *hasan*.

[20] Reported by Aboo Daawood [Eng. trans. 3/1312/no.3664] from Aboo Umaamah and its *isnaad* is *hasan*. It is reported by at-Tirmidhee (2521) and Ahmad [3/438,440]. So the *hadeeth* is *saheeh* by combination of its chains and witnesses.

[21] Reported by Muslim [Eng. trans. 1/37/no.96].

Obstacles in the Path of Loving for Allaah

O servant having love, know that loving for Allaah's sake is a rope which holds the hearts together through Allaah's light and guidance, the shade produced by it being mutual love, mercy, affection, visiting one another, and keeping ties of relationship for the sake of Allaah's Glory. But if one or the other commits a sin then it will cloud his heart and cause breakage in the connection with his companion's heart and cause separation which will be a fitting punishment for that sin.

He (ﷺ) said, *"There are no two persons who have mutual love for the sake of Allaah, the Mighty and Magnificent, or for Islaam, and then separation is caused between them except by a sin committed by one of them."*[24]

Therefore if a person finds some alienation from his brother then let him examine himself initially and if he finds that he is guilty of some sin then let him repent quickly and the love of his brother may be rectified.

---

[24] Reported by al-Bukhaaree in *al-Adaabul-Mufrad* (no.401). This *isnaad* is *hasan* and it has a witness from the *hadeeth* of Ibn 'Umar reported by Ahmad (2/68) and from the *hadeeth* of Aboo Hurairah reported by Aboo Nu'aim in *Hilyatul-Awliyaa'* (5/202), and the *hadeeth* is *saheeh* due to the combination of its supports and Allaah knows best.

What Should the Muslim Say when his Brother Informs him that he Loves him?

When the Muslim informs his brother that he loves him for Allaah's sake, then his brother should reply, "May the one for whose sake you have loved me, love you." (*ahabbakal-ladheee ahbabtanee feehi*)

Anas ibn Maalik said: *"A man passed by the Prophet (ﷺ) who was in the company of some people, so a man from those with him said, "Indeed I love that person for Allaah's sake." So the Prophet (ﷺ) said, "Have you informed him?" He said, "No." He (ﷺ) said, "Go to him and inform him." So he went to him and informed him, so he replied, "May the One for whose sake you have loved me love you." Then he returned and the Prophet (ﷺ) asked him and he told him what he had said. So the Prophet (ﷺ) said, "You will be with the one whom you have loved and there will be for you the reward that you hoped for."* [25]

---

[25] Reported by Aboo Daawood (Eng. trans 3/1419/no.5106), Ahmad (3/150), al-Haakim (4/171) and others. Its *isnaad* is *saheeh*.

He (ﷺ) said, *"The Deen is sincerity."* We said, *"To whom?"* He said, *"To Allaah, His Book, His Messenger and to the leaders of the Muslims and their common folk."*[27]

3) To keep the tie of relationship and to visit.

He (ﷺ) said, *"Visit from time to time - now and again - you will increase in love."*[28]

He (ﷺ) said, *"A man went to visit a brother of his in a another town and Allaah deputed an angel to await him on his way, so when he came to him he said, "Where are you going?" He replied, "I am going to visit a brother of mine in this town." He said, "Have you done him some favour which you desire to be returned?" He said, "No, it is just that I love him for Allaah, the Mighty and Magnificent." He said, "Then I am a messenger sent by Allaah to you (to inform you) that Allaah loves you as you have loved him for His sake."*[29]

So we know from these two noble *ahaadeeth* that visiting is something required by love, however it should be done in moderation, neither doing it too often, nor falling short, since visiting too often causes one to become weary of it, whereas falling short causes alienation and then cutting off of relations and we ask Allaah to keep us safe.

---

[27] Reported by Muslim [Eng. trans. 1/37/no.98] and others from the *hadeeth* of Tameem ad-Daaree, *radiyallaahu 'anhu*.

[28] *Saheeh*, reported by al-Bazzaar and others as has preceded.

[29] Reported by Muslim as has preceded.

Matters which Necessitate Hatred for Allaah's Sake

(1) *KUFR* (UNBELIEF)

Allaah, the Most High, says:

قَدْ كَانَتْ لَكُمْ أُسْوَةٌ حَسَنَةٌ فِي إِبْرَٰهِيمَ وَٱلَّذِينَ مَعَهُ إِذْ قَالُوا لِقَوْمِهِمْ
إِنَّا بُرَءَٰؤُا مِنكُمْ وَمِمَّا تَعْبُدُونَ مِن دُونِ ٱللَّهِ كَفَرْنَا بِكُمْ وَبَدَا بَيْنَنَا
وَبَيْنَكُمُ ٱلْعَدَٰوَةُ وَٱلْبَغْضَآءُ أَبَدًا حَتَّىٰ تُؤْمِنُوا بِٱللَّهِ وَحْدَهُ

"There is for you an excellent example (to follow) in Ibraaheem and those with him, when they said to their people, 'Verily, we are free from you and whatever you worship besides Allaah, we have rejected you, and there has arisen between us and you, hostility and hatred forever, until you believe in Allaah alone.'"

al-Mumtahinah (60):4

Allaah, the Most High, says:

لَّا تَجِدُ قَوْمًا يُؤْمِنُونَ بِٱللَّهِ وَٱلْيَوْمِ ٱلْأَخِرِ يُوَآدُّونَ مَنْ
حَآدَّ ٱللَّهَ وَرَسُولَهُ وَلَوْ كَانُوٓا ءَابَآءَهُمْ أَوْ أَبْنَآءَهُمْ
أَوْ إِخْوَٰنَهُمْ أَوْ عَشِيرَتَهُمْ

34

"You will not find any people who believe in Allaah and the Last Day, making friendship with those who oppose Allaah and His Messenger (ﷺ), even though they were their fathers, or their sons, or their brothers, or their kindred (people)."

al-Mujaadilah (58):22

This is the precise measure for *eemaan* in the souls. It is that the ranks of the Believers unite distinct and separate, free from every hindrance or enticement, and cling to the strongest handhold with a single rope.

Indeed Allaah has not given any man two hearts in his chest and man cannot unite the love of two (opposites) in his heart: the love of Allaah, His Messenger and the Believers - together with love of the enemies of Allaah, His Messenger and the Believers. He will have love of one and hatred of the other.

This is not a new affair, rather it has continued from the start of this *Ummah*, the *Ummah* of *Tawheed* and part of the same convoy - the convoy of *eemaan* stretching out through time, distinguished by *eemaan*, free from every connection contrary to the connection of *'aqeedah*.

The Muslim if he looks will see that he has an ancient and deep-rooted heritage, and an example which stretches back through the ages to Ibraaheem, the sincere worshipper of Allaah alone, free from shirk, so he will perceive that he has a store of experience behind him far greater than his personal experience, and far greater than the experience of his own generation.

(2) Hypocrisy (*Nifaaq*).

Allaah, the Most High, says:

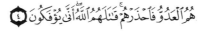

"They are the enemies, so beware of them. May Allaah curse them! How are they denying (or deviating from) the Right Path."

al-Munaafiqoon (63):4

Allaah, the One free of all deficiencies, has affirmed that the hypocrites are the first enemies to the Muslim, therefore it is essential to hate and detest them for Allaah's sake since the believer cannot love his enemy and the enemy of Allaah.

This hatred and detesting of them is emphasised by Allaah's invocation against them, and this is a decree that cannot be prevented by anyone nor changed.

(3) INNOVATING IN ALLAAH'S *DEEN*.

I have fully explained this in my book *Innovation (Bid'ah) and its evil effects upon the Ummah*

(4) SINS

Whoever commits any foul action has done that which is hated by Allaah, so the believing servant must hate his action and advise him and not be an aid of Shaitaan against him.

Al-Manaawee said in *Faydul-Qadeer* (3/69): "From hating for Allaah's sake is to hate many of those who ascribe themselves to knowledge in our time, due to the clear signs of hypocrisy visible upon them, and their hatred of the good people. So whoever has a heart free from sickness must hate them for the sake of Allaah for their arrogance, their evil manners and the harm they cause to the people."

12

Matters which do not Conflict with Hating for Allaah's Sake

Know, O brother in *eemaan*, that those who take the affair of hating for Allaah's sake and apply it unrestrictedly, not knowing where exceptions lie, will fall into error.

Here we quote a number of exceptions which do not contradict or conflict with hating for Allaah's sake, and they are not to be counted as belonging to love for Allaah's sake.

(1) MILDNESS IN PRESENTING AND PROPAGATING THE *DA'WAH.*

Hating for Allaah's sake does not mean withholding the call to Islaam or sincere advise from others and leaving them in the quagmire of sin, without giving them admonition or warning. Rather it is essential to order the good and forbid the evil, and to desire the guidance of those astray, and to have concern for them, and to have the sincere wish that they will enter obedience to Allaah and guidance.

Since this cannot be achieved except by affecting their souls, Allaah, the Most High, has made the milestones of the call to His way: Wisdom (*al-hikmah*), wise preaching (*al-maw'izatul-hasanah*) and debating in the best manner (*al-jidaal billatee hiya ahsan*).

Allaah, the Most High, says:

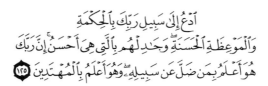

"Invite (all) to the Way of your Lord with wisdom and fair preaching, and argue with them in a way that is better. Truly, your Lord knows best who has gone astray from His Path, and He is Best Aware of those who are guided."

an-Nahl (16):125

Know, O Muslim, that straying souls and hardened hearts will not be softened except by displaying kindness, sympathy and concern. Therefore the instruction given to Moosa and Haaroon by Allaah when He sent them to the *Taaghoot* of Egypt, its Fir'awn, was:

أَذْهَبْ أَنتَ وَأَخُوكَ بِتَايَتِي وَلَا تَنِيَا فِي ذِكْرِى ۝ اذْهَبَا إِلَىٰ فِرْعَوْنَ إِنَّهُ طَغَىٰ ۝ فَقُولَا لَهُ قَوْلًا لَّيِّنًا لَّعَلَّهُ يَتَذَكَّرُ أَوْ يَخْشَىٰ ۝

"Go you and your brother with my Signs, and do not, you both, slacken and become weak in My Remembrance. Go, both of you, to Pharaoh, verily, he has transgressed. And *speak to him mildly*, perhaps he may accept admonition or fear Allaah."

Taa-Haa (20):42-44

This *Aayah* and its like do not contradict the saying of Allaah, the Most High:

يَتَأَيُّهَا النَّبِيُّ جَهِدِ الْكُفَّارَ وَالْمُنَفِقِينَ وَاغْلُظْ عَلَيْهِمْ وَمَأْوَىٰهُمْ جَهَنَّمُ وَبِئْسَ الْمَصِيرُ ۝

"O Prophet (Muhammad (ﷺ)) strive hard against the disbelievers and the hypocrites, and be harsh against them, their abode is Hell - indeed that is the worst destination."

at-Tawbah (9):73

This is because the harshness ordered is to be applied in two situations:
Firstly, when fighting: which of course needs vehemence and harshness, as Allaah, the Magnificent, says:

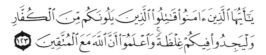

"O you who believe! Fight those of the disbelievers who are close to you, and let them find harshness in you, and know that Allaah is with those who are pious."

at-Tawbah (9):123

Secondly, when replying to the unbelievers whom the true call has reached and they have rejected it, and the people of innovation and evil and misleading ideas who prevent people from the true way, Allaah, the Most High, says:

وَإِذَا قِيلَ لَهُمْ تَعَالَوْا إِلَى مَا أَنزَلَ
ٱللَّهُ وَإِلَى ٱلرَّسُولِ رَأَيْتَ ٱلْمُنَفِقِينَ يَصُدُّونَ عَنكَ
صُدُودًا ۞ فَكَيْفَ إِذَا أَصَبَتْهُم مُّصِيبَةٌ بِمَا
قَدَّمَتْ أَيْدِيهِمْ ثُمَّ جَاءُوكَ يَحْلِفُونَ بِٱللَّهِ إِنْ أَرَدْنَا إِلَّا
إِحْسَنًا وَتَوْفِيقًا ۞ أُوْلَئِكَ ٱلَّذِينَ يَعْلَمُ ٱللَّهُ مَا
فِي قُلُوبِهِمْ فَأَعْرِضْ عَنْهُمْ وَعِظْهُمْ وَقُل لَّهُمْ فِي
أَنفُسِهِمْ قَوْلًا بَلِيغًا ۞

"And when it is said to them: 'Come to what Allaah has sent down to the Messenger,' you (Muhammad (ﷺ)) see the hypocrites turn away from you with aversion. How then, when a catastrophe befalls them because of what their hands have sent forth, they come to you swearing by Allaah, 'We meant no more than goodwill and conciliation!' They (the hypocrites) are those of whom Allaah knows what is in their hearts; so turn aside from them (do not punish them) but admonish them, and speak to them an effective word (i.e. to believe in Allaah, worship Him, obey Him, and be afraid of Him) to reach their innerselves."

an-Nisaa (4):61-63

Therefore the Messenger of Allaah (ﷺ) established a *minbar* for Hassaan to stand upon and ridicule the *mushriks* in poetry, and when Kisraa tore up the letter sent to him by Allaah's Messenger (ﷺ) calling him to Allaah - Allaah's Messenger (ﷺ) made supplication against him, and the proofs in this regard are many.

So with this the mistake of some scholars becomes apparent, those who claim that calling to Allaah is a matter for mildness whatever the case and that harshness is only to be used when fighting. If this were the case then the Messenger (ﷺ) should have fought and killed the hypocrites just as he did with the *mushriks*, however this was not the case. So it becomes clear that harshness extends also to include replying to them and explaining their falsehood, and rebutting the doubts they cause, and crushing their innovations, and this was the practice of the pious predecessors (*as-Salafus-Saaliheen*).

Know, O brother in *eemaan*, that this is a precise matter requiring careful consideration, that you may take the support of that which is firmly established.

Furthermore the one granted obedience to his Lord and who follows the *Sunnah* of His Messenger (ﷺ) should know that mildness in giving *da'wah* does not mean flattery or fawning, nor compromising anything from the *Deen*, nor watering Islaam down so that it agrees with people's whims and desires using the excuse that you are making things easy for the people. Nor does harshness, with the use of proof and strong words mean abusing, reviling or ignorant attacks.

(2) GOOD TREATMENT OF AN UNBELIEVER WITH WHOM THERE IS AN ISLAMIC PEACE TREATY, AND OF THE PERSON OF THE BOOK LIVING UNDER ISLAMIC RULE AS A *DHIMMEE*.

Allaah, the Most High, says:

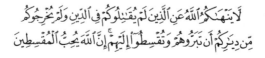

"Allaah does not forbid you to deal justly and kindly with those who fought not against you on account of religion and did not drive you out of your homes. Verily, Allaah loves those who deal with equity."

al-Mumtahinah (60):8

Conclusion

Know, O brother for the sake of Allaah, that loving and hating for Allaah's sake is the lofty apex at the head of the completion of *eemaan*, towards it gaze those who vie in loving Allaah and His Messenger (ﷺ), and the hearts of those who seek after the shade on the Day when there is no shade but His, the Most Perfect and the Most High, after they have been scorched by worldly connections.

Therefore, O brother in *eemaan* devote yourself to being one amongst those who have mutual love for Allaah's sake, and who form ties for Allaah's sake and exert their energies in that for Allaah's sake, those who will be envied by the prophets and the martyrs.

"O Allaah I declare that you are free from any imperfection and all praise is due to You, I bear witness that none has the right to be worshipped but You. I ask for Your forgiveness and I turn in repentance to You."

Glossary

Aayah (pl. Aayaat): a Sign of Allaah; a verse of the Qur'aan.

Aayaat: See *Aayah*.

Aboo (Abee, Abaa): father of; used as a means of identification..

Ahaadeeth: See *Hadeeth*.

'Aqeedah: that which binds or that which is rooted in the heart; firm belief; the beliefs and principles which one is upon.

Companions (Ar. *Sahaabah*): the Muslims who saw the Prophet (ﷺ) and died upon Islaam.

Da'eef: weak; unauthentic (narration).

Da'wah: invitation; call to Islaam.

Deen: way of life prescribed by Allaah i.e. Islaam.

Dhimmee: a non-Muslim living under the protection of the Islamic rule.

Eemaan: faith; to affirm all that was revealed to the Messenger (ﷺ), affirming with the heart, testifying with the tongue and acting with the limbs. The actions of the limbs are from the completeness of *Eemaan*. Faith increases with obedience to Allaah and decreases with disobedience.

Fir'awn: Pharaoh.

Hadeeth (pl. Ahaadeeth): narration concerning the utterances of the Prophet (ﷺ), his actions or an attribute of his.

Hasan: fine; term used for an authentic *hadeeth*, which does not reach the higher category of *Saheeh*.

Ibn: son of; used as a means of identification.

Imaam: leader; leader in *Salaah*, knowledge or *fiqh*; leader of a state.

Isnaad: the chain of narrators linking the collector of the saying to the person quoted.

Kufr: Disbelief.

Minbar: pulpit.

Mushrik: one who worships others along with Allaah or ascribes one or more of Allaah's attributes to other than Him; one who commits *shirk*.

Nifaaq: hypocrisy.

Radiyallaahu 'anhu/'anhaa/'anhum/'anhumaa: may Allaah be pleased with him/her/them/both of them.

Rahimahullaah/Rahimahumullaah: may Allaah bestow His mercy upon him/them.

Saheeh: correct; an authentic narration.

Salaf: predecessors; the early Muslims; the Muslims of the first three generations: the *Companions*, the *Successors* and their successors.

Salafus-Saaliheen: pious predecessors; the Muslims of the first three generations: the *Companions*, the *Successors* and their successors.

Shaikh: scholar.

Shaitaan: Satan.

Sharee'ah: the Divine code of Law.

Shirk: Associating partners with Allaah; compromising any category of *tawheed*.

Sunnah: in its broadest sense, the entire *Deen* which the Prophet (ﷺ) came with and taught, i.e. all matters of belief, rulings, manners and actions which were conveyed by the *Companions*. It also includes those matters which the Prophet (ﷺ) established by his sayings, actions and tacit approval - as opposed to *bid'ah* (innovation).

sunnah: an action of the Prophet (ﷺ).

Soorah: a chapter of the Qur'aan.

Taaghoot: one who goes beyond the limits (set by Allaah); one who is worshipped besides Allaah and is pleased with it.

Taqwa: obedience to Allaah by doing that which He ordered hoping for His reward and avoiding that which He forbade, fearing His punishment.

Tawheed: Allaah is the only Lord of creation, He alone, is their Provider and Sustainer, Allaah has Names and Attributes that none of the creation share and Allaah is to be singled out for worship, alone. Tawheed is maintaining the Oneness of Allaah in all the above mentioned categories. Islaam makes a clear distinction between the Creator and the created.

Ummah: "nation"; the Muslims as a group.